For Didi. I hope you'll always keep playing.

—E.I.H.

As an Asian immigrant, I am dedicating this book not only to immigrants throughout the United States but also to my fellow immigrants, Ferrari and Tanta.

—K.K.

Text © 2024 Emily Inouye Huey
Illustrations © 2024 Kaye Kang

Visit us at shadowmountain.com

Library of Congress Cataloging-in-Publication Data

(CIP data on file)

ISBN 978-1-63993-208-5

Printed in China   9/2023
RR Donnelley, Dongguan, China

10   9   8   7   6   5   4   3   2   1

WAT KEPT PLAYING

THE INSPIRING STORY OF WATARU MISAKA AND HIS RISE TO THE NBA

WRITTEN BY **EMILY INOUYE HUEY** • ILLUSTRATED BY **KAYE KANG**

SHADOW
MOUNTAIN
PUBLISHING

In an apartment below his father's barber shop, Wataru Misaka grew up loving both his Japanese heritage and his home country, the United States of America.

But Wat didn't always feel loved back. It seemed some people thought a person couldn't be both Japanese *and* American.

Yet Wat thought it was possible. When he played basketball, his worn sneakers skidding on a dirt court, Wat was just another player. When he passed the ball, snapping it from his hands to the next boy's, Wat was part of a team. And when he launched a high-arcing shot that *saaaaaailed*, then *swished*, the look on his friends' faces told Wat he was something else!

So Wat practiced. He dribbled. *Tha-dump, tha-dump*. He rebounded. *Ka-bang*. He shot. *Whoosh*. Sometimes, Wat practiced with his friends. Other times, he practiced alone. Always, Wat kept playing.

Then, on a clear December morning, Wat listened to an emergency radio broadcast: Japanese airplanes had dropped bombs on US military ships stationed in Hawaii. Wat couldn't understand why his grandparents' country would attack *his* country. Still, the next day, he and his Japanese American classmates were turned away from school.

Japan and the United States were now at war. Fear and anger roiled through the country. More than 120,000 Japanese Americans, mostly from communities on the West Coast, were forced out of their homes and into prison camps.

Wat's family was allowed to stay
in their home in Ogden, Utah, but
they still faced prejudice.

Wat didn't understand. Why were his Japanese friends being imprisoned? Why were people he'd never met afraid of him? *Was* it possible to be both Japanese and American?

When the questions didn't seem to have answers, Wat turned to basketball.
Tha-dump, tha-dump, ka-bang, whoosh. Wat kept playing.

Two years passed. Wat earned a spot in the engineering program at the University of Utah. While on campus, Wat saw flyers advertising tryouts for the basketball team. With the war still going, he knew some people wouldn't like seeing him on the court, but he decided to give it his best shot.

At only five foot seven, Wat was shorter than every other player on the court. However, they soon found out that he could play. "Fast. Likable. Good defender. A team player. A leader." The team immediately saw what their newest forward had to offer.

They also saw—some for the first time—the racism that Wat had dealt with his whole life. Crowds booed when Wat walked onto the court. A referee called unfair fouls against him. The team watched as Wat turned his back to the hecklers. He ignored the ugly jeers, listening instead to the rhythms of the game. *Tha-dump, tha-dump, ka-bang, whoosh*. Wat kept playing.

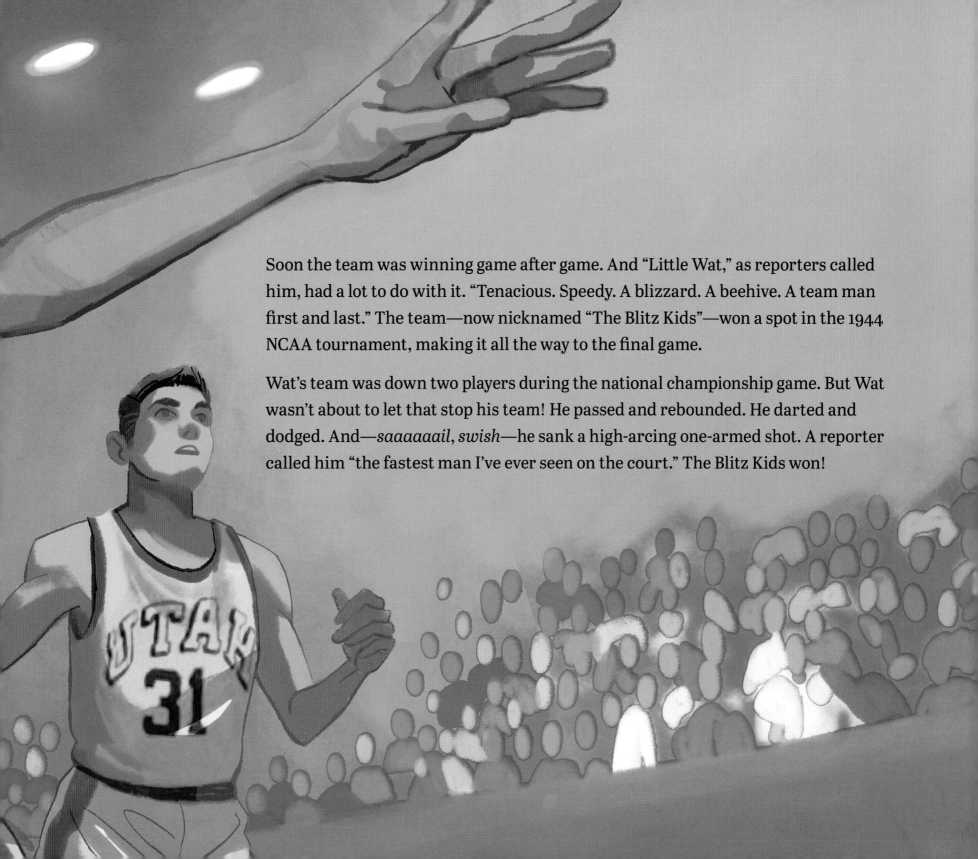

Soon the team was winning game after game. And "Little Wat," as reporters called him, had a lot to do with it. "Tenacious. Speedy. A blizzard. A beehive. A team man first and last." The team—now nicknamed "The Blitz Kids"—won a spot in the 1944 NCAA tournament, making it all the way to the final game.

Wat's team was down two players during the national championship game. But Wat wasn't about to let that stop his team! He passed and rebounded. He darted and dodged. And—*saaaaaail, swish*—he sank a high-arcing one-armed shot. A reporter called him "the fastest man I've ever seen on the court." The Blitz Kids won!

Wat felt about as good as he ever had—until the team pulled into the train station back in Utah. Wat's mother held an official notice. The United States was calling him to war. For the first time ever, Wat hung up his sneakers.

Wat was sent to Japan, entering Hiroshima just months after the United States had dropped the first atomic bomb on the city. Wat's job was to interview Japanese civilians, but the Japanese feared Wat's US uniform. And the White American soldiers he worked with mistrusted Wat, who looked like the people they had been fighting. Wat wondered where he belonged. Was he Japanese or American? Sometimes, it felt as if neither country claimed him.

When the war ended, Wat returned to the University of Utah and went right back to playing basketball. After another stunning season, the Blitz Kids were invited to play in the NIT Championship—the biggest basketball tournament in the United States. They were going to New York City!

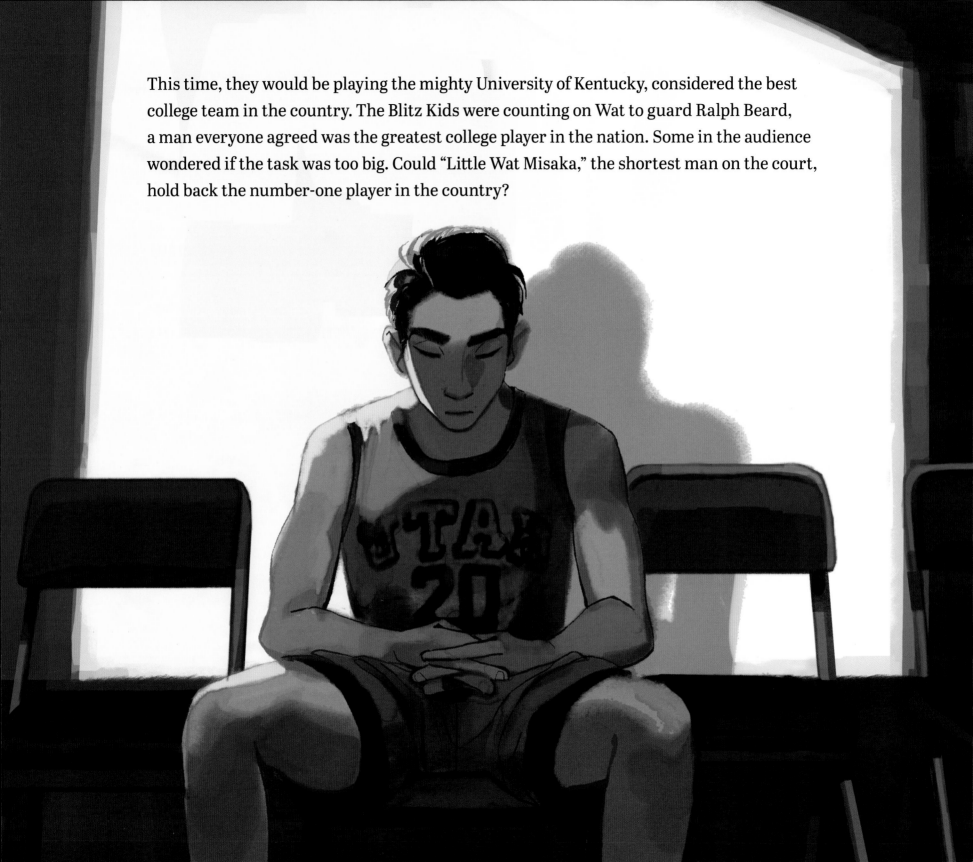

This time, they would be playing the mighty University of Kentucky, considered the best college team in the country. The Blitz Kids were counting on Wat to guard Ralph Beard, a man everyone agreed was the greatest college player in the nation. Some in the audience wondered if the task was too big. Could "Little Wat Misaka," the shortest man on the court, hold back the number-one player in the country?

Tha-dump, tha-dump, ka-bang, whoosh. Wat kept playing, letting the rhythms he'd practiced flow through his body. All night, he hustled, defending the floor, exactly where Ralph didn't want him to be. Reporters went wild: "A human spark plug." "Kilowatt." "Defensive whiz!" By the end of the night, Ralph had scored only one point.

Again, the Blitz Kids won!

Something was happening off the court as well. The crowd roared—cheering specifically for Wat! The New York crowd, full of people whose families were immigrants just like the Misakas, claimed Wat as one of their own. A reporter wrote, "No player ever got a bigger cheer!"

Wat swallowed as he looked around the stadium at the thousands of people who saw him for what he was: both Japanese *and* American—and an *amazing* ball player.

Several months later, Wat was drafted by the New York Knicks, becoming the first-ever person of color to play in the Basketball Association of America. And he wouldn't be the last.

There were still people who didn't understand Wat. He still sometimes faced prejudice. But Wat knew who he was. He loved being Japanese. He loved being an American.

And Wat kept playing.

AUTHOR'S NOTE

In 1947, only months after Jackie Robinson broke the color line in professional baseball and one year after the last Japanese American incarceration center was closed, Wataru Misaka was selected to play for the New York Knicks in the Basketball Association of America, which later became the NBA. He was the first person of color to play professional basketball. There was no celebration about his recruitment though. "It wasn't a big thing," he later said. "No one cared."

Wat played three games and scored seven points before being cut from the team. He never learned why he was cut. Some have speculated that his race was a factor, but others think the team simply had too many guards.

Wat was almost immediately invited to play for the Harlem Globetrotters, a professional team of Black American players segregated from the BAA. Wat had previously played against the Globetrotters in exhibition games and considered the team to be the best in the world at the time. But after some consideration, Wat declined and completed his engineering degree, which paid the same salary as the sports team. He received his bachelor's degree in 1948 and worked as an engineer until his retirement at the age of ninety-one.

Wat continued playing sports throughout his life, becoming an avid golfer and bowler. In 1997, he was inducted into the Japanese American Bowling Hall of Fame. In 1999, he was inducted into the Utah Sports Hall of Fame.

It was only later in his life that Wat was celebrated for his role in breaking pro basketball's color barrier. In 2009, he walked out to the center of Madison Square Garden and the Knicks honored his place in basketball history. That same year, President Barack Obama invited Wat to the White House, congratulating Wat for his "competitive spirit" and for being the "first non-white player in the NBA."

For more information about Wat Misaka, visit https://emilyhuey.com/.